...ts Behind

Medical Advances

Eve Hartman and Wendy Meshbesher

Chicago, Illinois

www.heinemannraintree.com
Visit our website to find out
more information about
Heinemann-Raintree books.

To order:
☎ Phone 888-454-2279
▤ Visit www.heinemannraintree.com
to browse our catalog and order online.

Edited by Andrew Farrow, Adam Miller, and
  Diyan Leake
Designed by Philippa Jenkins
Original illustrations © Capstone Global Library
  Limited 2011
Illustrated by Capstone Global Library Limited
Picture research by Hannah Taylor
Originated by Capstone Global Library Limited
Printed in the United States of America by
  Worzalla Publishing

14 13 12 11 10
10 9 8 7 6 5 4 3 2 1

Library of Congress Cataloging-in-Publication Data
  The scientists behind medical advances / Eve Hartman
and Wendy Meshbesher.
      p. cm.—(Sci-hi scientists)
  Includes bibliographical references and index.
  ISBN 978-1-4109-4048-3 (hc)—ISBN 978-1-4109-4055-1
(pb) 1. Medical scientists—Juvenile literature. 2. Medical
innovations—Juvenile literature. I. Meshbesher, Wendy.
II. Title.
  R134.H26 2011
  610—dc22   2010031263

Acknowledgments
The author and publishers are grateful to the following
for permission to reproduce copyright material:
Alamy Images p. **40** (© Picture Contact); The Art
Archive p. **5** (University Library Prague/Dagli Orti);
Corbis pp. **4** (ATC Productions), 7 (Hulton-Deutsch
Collection), **11** (Bettmann), **12** (Bettmann), **16** (Karen
Kasmauski), **17** (Gideon Mendel), **29** (Science Faction/
Library of Congress), **30** (Martin Philbey), **39** (Joseph
Sohm); Getty Images pp. **13** (Peter Kramer), **15** (The
Bridgeman Art Library), **19** bottom (Time Life Pictures/
Alfred Eisenstaedt), **20** (Popperfoto/Paul Popper), **27**
bottom (Jeoffrey Maitem), **28** (Popperfoto), 32 (Hulton
Archive); Photolibrary pp. **23**, **37** (Blend/Hill Street
Studios); Dr Koneru Satya Prasad/HEAL **contents page**
bottom, p. **36**; Reuters pp. **9** (Scanpix Scanpix), **25**
(Mike Hutchings); Rex Features pp. **27** top, **38** (Caroline
Mardon); Science Photo Library pp. **8** (Richard T. Nowitz),
14 (Jean-Loup Charmet), **22** (Volker Steger), **24**, **26**
(National Library of Medicine), **33** (AJ Photo), **41** (Peter
Menzel); shutterstock background images and design
elements throughout, **contents page** top (© Li Wa), **19**
top (© Li Wa); Still Pictures p. **21** (Peter Arnold/Jim Olive);
University of Michigan Health System p. **31**; © Matthew
Williams p. **35**.

Main cover photograph of surgery reproduced with
permission of Photolibrary (BSIP Medical/B. Boissonnet);
inset cover photograph of a Petri dish with mould
reproduced with permission of shutterstock
(© Alexander Raths).

The publisher would like to thank literary consultants
Marla Conn and Nancy Harris and content consultant
Suzy Gazlay for their assistance in the preparation of
this book.

Every effort has been made to contact copyright holders
of material reproduced in this book. Any omissions will
be rectified in subsequent printings if notice is given to
the publisher.

Disclaimer
All the Internet addresses (URLs) given in this book were
valid at the time of going to press. However, due to the
dynamic nature of the Internet, some addresses may
have changed, or sites may have changed or ceased to
exist since publication. While the author and publisher
regret any inconvenience this may cause readers, no
responsibility for any such changes can be accepted by
either the author or the publisher.

Contents

Medical Science 4

Diseases from Germs 6

New Drugs 10

Vaccines 14

Surgery 18

More Amazing Surgery 22

Public Health 24

Cancer 28

Healthy Babies 32

Sports Medicine 34

Doctors Who Make a Difference 36

The Future of Medicine 40

Timeline 42

Glossary 44

Find Out More 46

Index 48

What is a blood bank? Find out on page 19!

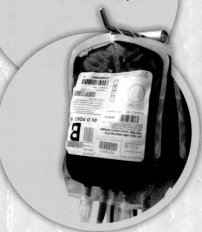

Who started HEAL? Turn to page 36 to find out!

Some words are shown in bold, **like this**. These words are explained in the glossary. You will find important information and definitions underlined, <u>like this</u>.

MEDICAL SCIENCE

Your body is an amazing machine. It pumps blood, breathes air, and digests food 24 hours a day. With proper training, you could use your body to climb a mountain, score a goal in soccer, or play a musical instrument.

However, the body can also suffer from diseases and injuries. It can easily recover from a mild cold or a scraped knee, but it needs help to recover from more serious illnesses or accidents. Medical doctors, or physicians, can and do provide this help. So can nurses and other health care providers.

Doctors and nurses apply their skills and new technology to help patients.

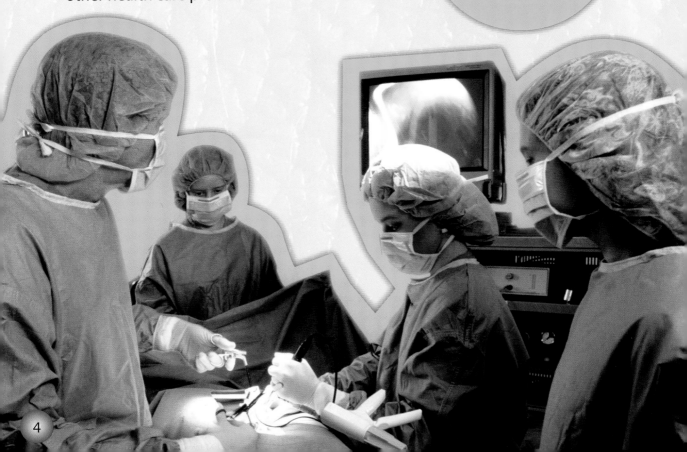

THE ART AND SCIENCE OF MEDICINE

In most places around the world today, the practice of medicine is based on science. Medical doctors train at medical schools for many years before beginning their practice.

Doctors understand nearly all diseases and injuries, and they can often cure or help people recover from illnesses. At many hospitals and universities, doctors continue to study diseases and ways to improve medicine. People everywhere benefit from their work.

This book presents the work of doctors and nurses, scientists, and others who have contributed to the practice of medicine. Many of these people lived in the past, and their work still matters. You also will read about doctors who are making a difference in communities around the world today.

OH NO! BAD MEDICINE

Hundreds of years ago, many diseases and injuries were fatal (caused death). The doctors and healers in those days did not understand the causes of many diseases. Sometimes a treatment they offered was worse than the disease itself. One common treatment was "bleeding" (draining off much of the body's blood). This sometimes killed the patient.

DISEASES FROM GERMS

Have you ever had a cold or flu? Maybe you have suffered from a sore throat, an ear infection, or tooth decay. **Germs** cause each of these illnesses, and some other very serious diseases, too. Throughout human history, germ-related diseases, such as **smallpox** and **cholera**, have caused huge numbers of deaths.

Germs are tiny living or nonliving things that can invade the body and cause harm. They include many **bacteria** and certain **fungi**, which are alive. They also include **viruses**, which are not alive. All germs are too small to see without a microscope. Smallpox and cholera are deadly diseases. Smallpox causes skin rashes and fever. Cholera affects the digestion.

KILLING GERMS

What happens to fruit, cheese, and other foods if you leave them on a table for too long? The answer is that they spoil (become rotten). The French scientist Louis Pasteur found a way to kill some germs that cause this to happen.

HELP FROM THE INSIDE?

Not all bacteria and fungi are harmful to humans. Many are not only helpful, but also necessary. For example, countless numbers of bacteria live inside your intestines. They help to break down the food you eat. They also prevent harmful bacteria from invading the intestines.

SEEING GERMS

In the 1670s, the Dutch scientist Anton van Leeuwenhoek built some of the first useful microscopes. With the aid of his inventions, he became the first person to observe and identify bacteria and other tiny organisms. Hundreds of years would pass, however, before scientists recognized that germs cause disease.

Pasteur studied many subjects, including math, chemistry, and physics. However, after two of his children died of typhoid fever, he devoted his life to finding cures for diseases. Other scientists had already suggested that germs cause diseases. Pasteur's experiments provided the evidence that convinced others of this idea.

Pasteur discovered that gentle heating could kill or slow the germs in milk and other beverages. Today, this process is called pasteurization in his honor. Pasteur also helped to develop **vaccines**, which are treatments to prevent germs from infecting the body.

1 Pasteur prepared two sealed flasks, each holding clear broth. He boiled the broth to kill the bacteria in them.

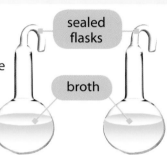

2 After a few days, the broth remained clear in both flasks. Pasteur broke the seal of one flask.

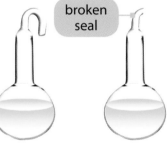

3 Days later, the broth in the sealed flask remained clear. The broth in the unsealed flask became brown and cloudy.

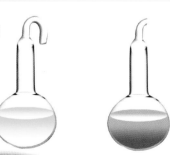

In one experiment, Pasteur used two glass flasks to prove that bacteria are in the air.

LOUIS PASTEUR

LIVED: 1822–1895

NATIONALITY: French

FAMOUS FOR: Proving that germs cause disease; finding a way to make stored milk safe to drink

DID YOU KNOW? Pasteur's father and grandfather were tanners. A tanner treats animal skins to make leather.

STOPPING GERMS NOW!

Today, all doctors recognize that germs can cause disease. They also know that germs are everywhere, including on food, clothing, and skin. This is why doctors regularly use gloves when examining a patient. It's also why operating rooms are kept completely **sterile** (germ free).

Many of the health habits you practice keep germs from infecting your body. These habits include brushing your teeth, taking a bath or shower, washing your hands, and cooking meat and other foods before eating them.

When bacteria do enter the body and cause disease, doctors often have medicine to help the body fight them. <u>Bacteria can be killed or slowed by drugs called **antibiotics**</u>.

The body is able to rid itself of many viral infections, such as the common cold and mild cases of flu. Other viral infections are more serious. One example is the virus known as **HIV**, which causes a deadly disease called **AIDS**. Researchers are still working to develop drugs and other treatments to fight AIDS.

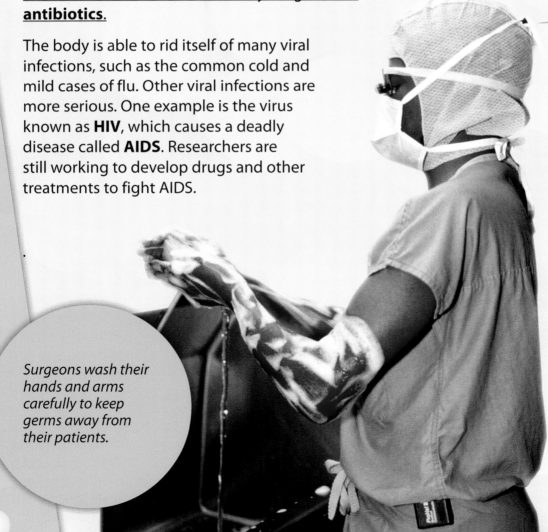

Surgeons wash their hands and arms carefully to keep germs away from their patients.

WHAT A PAIN!

Many adults suffer from a stomach **ulcer**. This is a break in the lining of the stomach or small intestine. It can be very painful. For years doctors thought that high levels of stomach acid caused ulcers. The Australian physician Barry Marshall proved this idea to be wrong. He identified that ulcers are caused by a type of bacteria.

In the 1980s, Marshall and his colleague Robin Warren developed the **hypothesis** (idea that can be tested) that bacteria causes ulcers.

A DARING TEST

To test his ideas, Marshall took the unusual step of using himself as a test subject. He drank a sample of fluids filled with the bacteria that he believed cause ulcers. Soon afterward he developed stomach pains, nausea, and began vomiting. After he took antibiotics that killed the bacteria, he recovered.

Marshall's work surprised many other doctors. Nevertheless, none could deny his results and conclusions. Marshall's work showed the power of science; that evidence and logic are more powerful than old opinions.

*Barry Marshall (left) and Robin Warren were awarded the **Nobel Prize** for showing that bacteria cause ulcers.*

NEW DRUGS

A **drug** or **medicine** is a substance that changes how the body functions. Where do drugs come from? In many cases they come from parts of living things. Aspirin, for example, came from the bark of willow trees. A heart medicine called digitalis comes from the foxglove, a type of wildflower.

USEFUL FUNGI

Fungi are a group of living things that includes mushrooms, **yeasts**, and molds. Not many scientists thought that fungi could prove useful as medicines. But that's exactly what Scottish scientist Alexander Fleming found in 1928.

Fleming discovered a medicine called **penicillin** almost by accident. He was growing bacteria in a special dish in his laboratory. The dish became contaminated (spoiled) by a spore of *Penicillium*, a type of fungus. The spore (part that grows into a new fungus) may have drifted in from elsewhere in the building.

Fleming might easily have thrown away the contaminated dish. Instead, he observed it carefully. Fleming saw that the bacteria around the fungus in the dish were dying. He concluded that the fungus was making a substance that was killing the bacteria. Soon he isolated the substance and called it penicillin.

Penicillin was the first antibiotic. As you read earlier, an antibiotic is a drug that kills bacteria. Penicillin became an important medicine against all sorts of bacterial infections.

PENICILLIN FOR EVERYONE

Fleming discovered penicillin, but two other scientists worked out how to make it useful. Howard Florey and Ernst Chain reviewed Fleming's work. Then they tested several methods of making the drug in large amounts. By discovering new *Penicillium* fungi and treating them with X-rays, they increased production of the drug by 1,000 times. For their work, Fleming, Florey, and Chain all received the Nobel Prize for Medicine.

Severe wounds often are infected. In World War II (1939–1945), penicillin saved the lives of many injured soldiers.

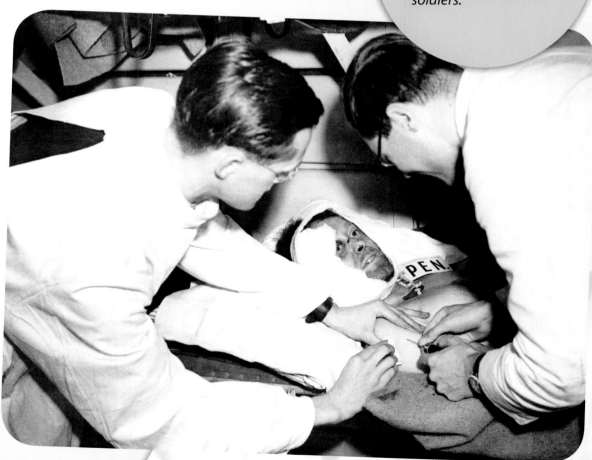

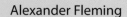Alexander Fleming
Ernst Chain
Howard Florey

ALEXANDER FLEMING

LIVED:	1881–1955
NATIONALITY:	Scottish
FAMOUS FOR:	Discovering penicillin, the first antibiotic
DID YOU KNOW?	Fleming was made an honorary chief of the Kiowa tribe, a group of Native Americans.

THE NEED FOR NEW DRUGS

Today, researchers at universities and drug companies continue to develop new drugs. Many serious diseases are difficult or impossible to treat with the drugs now available. Other drugs are very expensive to make or obtain, and less expensive versions would be useful.

Drug companies must also replace older antibiotics, such as the original form of penicillin. The reason is that, <u>over time, bacteria develop resistance to (cannot be killed by) any antibiotic that is widely used.</u> The version of penicillin that Fleming discovered, for example, is no longer effective. Newer antibiotics have replaced it. In time, bacteria will develop resistance to them, too.

Where can scientists search for new drugs? One place is a rain forest. A rain forest is a hot, wet, and dense forest found in Africa, South America, and Asia. A huge number and variety of plants and animals live in the rain forest. Many plants make **chemicals** (substances) to protect themselves from animals that might eat them. These chemicals might be useful as drugs.

Grace Gobbo studies the plants of the rain forest to find new medicines. She also talks to the people who live in the rain forests. Many of the elders (older, respected people) know which rain forest plants can help cure diseases. Gobbo's goal is to preserve their knowledge and share it with the rest of the world.

Unfortunately, much of the world's rain forest lands are disappearing. People are cutting them down to build new cities, farms, and ranches. Scientists like Grace Gobbo hope to preserve the rain forests, both for their value as forests and for the medicine-producing plants and animals they contain.

GRACE GOBBO

BORN:	1974
NATIONALITY:	Tanzanian
FAMOUS FOR:	Researching new medicines in rain forests
DID YOU KNOW?	One of Gobbo's heroes is Jane Goodall, an expert on chimpanzees.

Jane Goodall

Grace Gobbo

Vaccines

Until the early 1900s, a disease called smallpox claimed hundreds of thousands of lives every year. No one on Earth has suffered from smallpox for at least 30 years. The World Health Organization claims that the disease has been totally removed from the human population. No one will ever suffer from it again!

How was this feat accomplished? The answer is a kind of treatment called a vaccine. A vaccine is made from dead or weakened bacteria or viruses. When a vaccine is injected into a person's body, the body learns to fight the bacteria or virus without getting ill. This prevents a real infection from occurring.

EDWARD JENNER

LIVED:	1749–1823
NATIONALITY:	British
FAMOUS FOR:	Developing vaccines
DID YOU KNOW?	Jenner was appointed physician to King George IV of England. He was also made mayor of Berkley, his home town in Gloucestershire, England.

EARLY VACCINES

The idea of a vaccine was tried, with some success, at many times in human history. But Edward Jenner was the first to develop a working vaccine, prove it was successful, and bring vaccines to the general public. Today he is credited for saving more lives than anyone else in history.

In Jenner's time, smallpox was killing or maiming huge numbers of people. Jenner noticed that people who worked with cows did not catch smallpox. Instead they got cowpox, a much milder form of the disease. This proved to be the key to Jenner's discovery.

COWPOX: THE FIRST VACCINE

In the late 1700s, Jenner formed the hypothesis that cowpox provided immunity (protection) from smallpox. He tested the hypothesis by injecting a young boy with a source of cowpox. The boy became mildly ill. Later, he exposed the same boy to smallpox. The boy did not become ill.

The cowpox injection became the first vaccine. In the years that followed, people around the world received the vaccine and were protected from smallpox. Jenner's work did not cure the deadly disease, but it did help stop it from spreading.

This is an artist's impression showing Jenner (in the black coat) injecting his test subject with cowpox taken from the milkmaid on the far right.

VACCINES TODAY

Vaccines now prevent diseases such as measles, polio, diphtheria, and rubella. These were all once common, but are now much more rare. Vaccines are also available for flu viruses. Sometimes flu can be very serious.

Researchers continue to search for new vaccines, especially for serious diseases such as malaria and AIDS. One problem that researchers face is that viruses can mutate, or change. Vaccines often work only on specific parts of a virus. <u>If a virus mutates, a vaccine against it may no longer be effective.</u>

Today, vaccines against many diseases are widely used around the world.

AIDS

Beginning in the 1980s, doctors began to observe a new disease among their patients. The disease was named acquired immune deficiency syndrome, or AIDS. AIDS weakens the human body's immune system, which is the system that fights infections. As AIDS progresses, the patient becomes weaker and weaker, and eventually dies.

AIDS is now a serious disease all over the world, especially in Africa. Over 25 million people have died of AIDS. Millions more suffer from the disease.

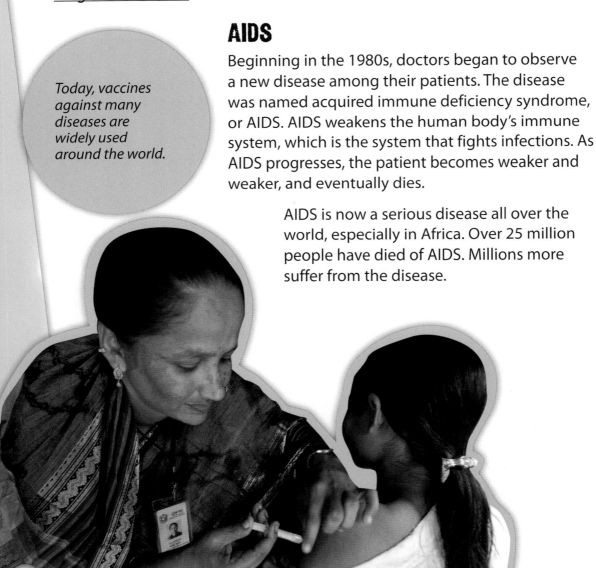

Patients with HIV await treatment at an AIDS clinic in South Africa.

HIV: THE VIRUS THAT CAUSES AIDS

The cause of AIDS is a virus called human immunodeficiency virus, or HIV. Scientists are looking for a reliable vaccine against HIV, but the task has proved difficult.

HIV can be transmitted from person to person through sexual contact or blood transfusions. It cannot be transmitted through casual contact, such as a handshake or kiss.

DR. LINDA-GAIL BEKKER

Dr. Linda-Gail Bekker helps to run an AIDS clinic in Cape Town, South Africa. Her clinic participates in the HIV Trials Network, a team of scientists from around the world. Dr. Bekker and her team believe that the key to finding an effective AIDS vaccine is for researchers to work together and share information.

Surgery

In many cases, medicine alone cannot cure a disease. Many serious conditions, such as a ruptured appendix, need to be dealt with promptly for a patient to survive. During **surgery**, a doctor opens a patient's body and treats or repairs a faulty organ, such as the heart or lungs. In hospitals all over the world, surgeons save or improve a huge number of lives every day.

WOUND INFECTION

Up until the 1800s, surgery was often extremely risky for the patient. Wounds from surgery often became infected. Doctors had a very poor understanding of infection and how to treat it.

As you read on page 7, Louis Pasteur helped to prove the existence of germs. The British surgeon Joseph Lister paid careful attention to Pasteur's work. Lister began several practices to reduce the invasion of germs during his operations. He treated surgical instruments with germ-killing chemicals. He also washed his hands before surgery and wore gloves.

Lister's efforts proved very successful. <u>Today, hospitals insist that surgery be performed under antiseptic (germ-free) conditions</u>. This reduces the risk of infection.

JOSEPH LISTER

LIVED:	1827–1912
NATIONALITY:	British
FAMOUS FOR:	Showing that cleanliness prevented infections during surgery
DID YOU KNOW?	Listerine, a brand of mouthwash, was named in Lister's honor.

BLOOD BANKS

Patients often lose blood during surgery. If someone is seriously injured, they may lose blood as part of their injury. A physician named Charles Drew helped to develop **blood banks**, which are sites for storing blood. At a blood bank, a donor's blood can be saved until a patient needs it. Drew's work helped to save the lives of many soldiers during World War II.

Drew, an African American, argued that blood could be donated and received regardless of a person's race or ethnic background. Scientists now recognize that this is correct.

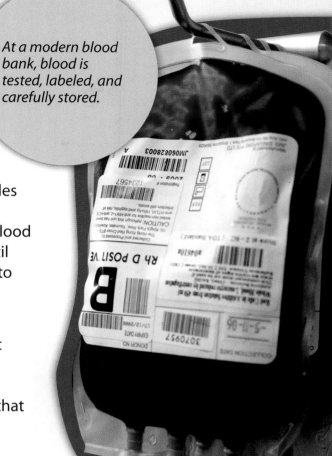

At a modern blood bank, blood is tested, labeled, and carefully stored.

CHARLES DREW

LIVED: 1904–1950

NATIONALITY: American

FAMOUS FOR: Blood banks

DID YOU KNOW? Drew played for his college football team, and was voted most valuable player.

GROUNDBREAKING SURGERY

Just what kinds of things can surgery accomplish? The list grows longer every day! Surgeons are now able to work on every organ of the human body, including the heart, brain, liver, and intestines. Surgeons can cut away a diseased section of intestine, then sew the remaining ends together. They can cut out cancerous **tumors**, which are clumps of potentially fatal growths on an organ. They can even repair a hole in the wall of a heart!

A DIFFICULT PROCEDURE

How can a diseased heart be removed and replaced without killing the patient? In 1967 Dr. Christiaan Barnard solved this puzzle when he completed the first successful human-to-human heart transplant. The operation took over 9 hours and involved a team of 30 people. Although the patient lived for only 18 days after surgery, the operation showed that a heart transplant was possible.

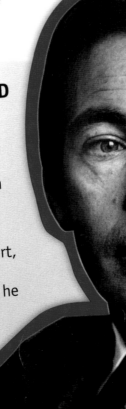

CHRISTIAAN BARNARD

LIVED:	1922–2001
NATIONALITY:	South African
FAMOUS FOR:	Performing the first human heart transplant
DID YOU KNOW?	After he successfully transplanted a human heart, Barnard became a world celebrity. People thought he looked like a movie star!

Barnard continued performing heart transplant surgeries. One patient lived for over 23 years with his new heart, which is still longer than typical results. Barnard also pioneered a type of surgery in which a new heart is added without removing the original heart. Ideally, the new heart helps the original heart to recover.

Today, surgeons worldwide perform thousands of heart transplants every year. The new hearts may come from a human donor or an animal donor. Sometimes artificial hearts are used.

THE REMARKABLE HEART

The heart pumps blood throughout the body. In a healthy adult, the heart typically beats about 60 to 80 times a minute. If the heart stopped beating, the body would quickly die.

Artificial hearts like this one have been used as transplants since 1982.

MORE AMAZING SURGERY

Transplants are only one example of the incredible surgery that surgeons can now offer. Here are some more examples.

Artificial limbs

Sometimes people lose a hand or other limb due to an accident or disease. In the past, the best that doctors could offer was a replacement limb made of wood or plastic. Today, the replacements are much improved.

The artificial hand shown in the photo performs movements like a real hand. It can grasp a wide range of objects. Its movements are flexible and its grasp is never too hard or soft. The surface of the hand is soft to the touch, making it feel more natural. It is also lightweight and cheap to produce.

To install an artificial limb, a surgeon must attach it in just the right position in relation to the patient's existing bones and muscles.

BRAIN SURGERY

Like any other organ, the brain can suffer from disease or injury. However, operations on the brain are often difficult because the brain is so vital to the human body. In addition, many parts of the brain are extremely difficult for a surgeon to reach.

Today, brain surgeons are able to treat a wide variety of injuries and diseases to the human brain. They can remove tumors, drain fluid that builds up on the brain, and repair injured blood vessels that supply the brain. Researchers continue to look for ways to improve brain surgery.

EYE SURGERY

The structures of the eye are among the smallest and most delicate of the human body. To perform surgery on the eye, doctors often use lasers. Lasers are a type of very precise light. Certain powerful lasers can be used as cutting tools.

With the help of lasers and other technology, eye surgeons are able to improve the vision of many patients with a simple and safe operation. Many operations are now possible only because of lasers.

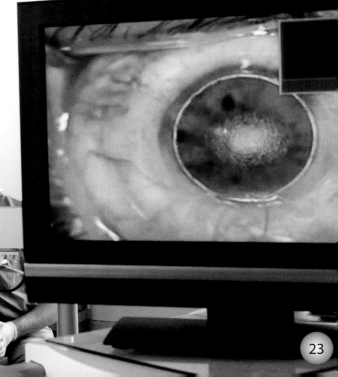

PUBLIC HEALTH

Beginning in the 1800s, new industries and technology meant that people started living closely together in large cities. The cramped conditions created many health problems. One of these was a rise in cholera, a disease that strikes the digestive tract. Victims of cholera lose water rapidly and often die within a few days.

Today, scientists know that cholera is caused by bacteria. This was not known in the 1800s, when cholera often spread quickly and suddenly. In 1854 an outbreak of cholera in London killed 500 people in about ten days! Cholera killed over 3,000 people in Chicago that same year.

JOHN SNOW

LIVED:	1813–1858
NATIONALITY:	British
FAMOUS FOR:	His groundbreaking study in the field of public health
DID YOU KNOW?	Snow was also a specialist in **anesthesia** (pain relief). He gave pain-relieving drugs to Queen Victoria when she gave birth to the last two of her nine children.

PROMOTING PUBLIC HEALTH

Most doctors at the time believed that cholera was caused by bad air. The British physician John Snow doubted this. He turned his attention to the water supply of London.

Snow talked to residents and looked at the numbers of people who had become ill. He concluded that the source of the cholera outbreak was a single water pump in Soho, London. He helped to prove this by plotting the cases of cholera on a map of London. The cases were clustered around that pump! It was later discovered that the pump had been contaminated by a cesspit (dump for human waste and other sewage).

The work of Snow and others showed the importance of clean water for good public health. As cities began to improve their sewers and public water supplies, diseases such as cholera declined.

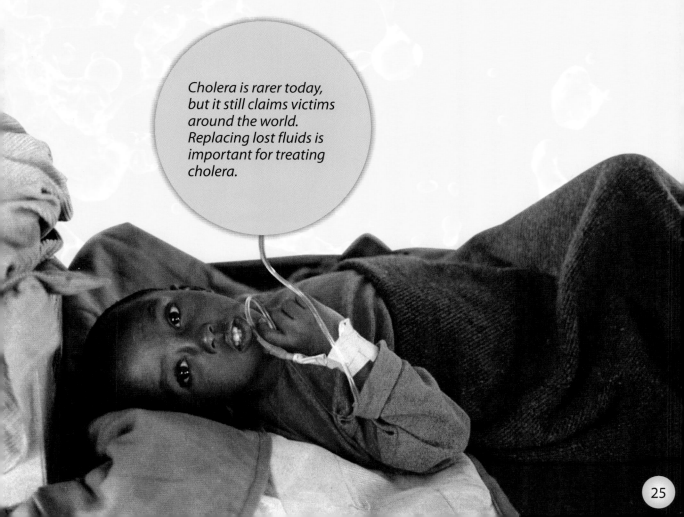

Cholera is rarer today, but it still claims victims around the world. Replacing lost fluids is important for treating cholera.

PUBLIC HEALTH TODAY

Thanks to improved public health, cholera no longer troubles many people. Yet other diseases still claim many lives, and public health officials work to slow or stop them. Their jobs include inspecting restaurants and cafeterias to make sure food is prepared safely. They also inspect water treatment plants to make sure water supplies are free of germs. They may help distribute vaccines, research new diseases, and keep people informed about diseases and how to prevent them.

What is the biggest public health problem today? The likely answer is poverty. The world's poor often lack nutritious food, clean water, and proper housing. They may rarely, if ever, see a doctor or nurse. Improving the health of poor people is an important step in improving their lives.

JANET LANE-CLAYPON

One of the founders of the study of public health was a British doctor, Janet Lane-Claypon (1877–1967). During her career, she worked to improve the health of mothers and their babies. Many of her ideas remain accepted today.

In one famous experiment, Lane-Claypon showed the benefits of breast-feeding for newborn babies. One group of babies was fed cow's milk, and the other group was fed milk from their mothers. The babies fed with their mothers' milk gained more weight and were healthier.

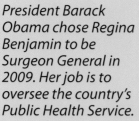

President Barack Obama chose Regina Benjamin to be Surgeon General in 2009. Her job is to oversee the country's Public Health Service.

DOCTORS WITHOUT BORDERS

Doctors Without Borders is an international organization of doctors, nurses, and other health care professionals. All are committed to a single idea: that everyone in the world is entitled to health care. They now treat people in over 70 countries. They treat civilians (nonfighting people) who are injured in wars, victims of natural disasters, and poor people who have no other access to health care.

In 1999 Doctors Without Borders received the **Nobel Prize** for peace.

Cancer

The human body is made of a huge number of **cells**. Cells are the smallest units that make up all living things. Cells divide to make new cells all the time. Usually this process occurs in an orderly, useful manner.

In the disease called cancer, cells divide quickly and in a harmful manner. They may form a mass of diseased cells called a tumor. Different types of cancer may strike or spread to nearly every organ of the body. Today, many forms of cancer can be treated effectively. The treatments may involve medicine, surgery, and radiation (a type of energy that travels in waves).

CHEMICAL TREATMENT

Paul Ehrlich began his career studying dyes and stains. However, he is most remembered for using chemicals to treat disease, an idea he called **chemotherapy**. Ehrlich's goal was to find chemicals that would travel through the blood and affect only diseased cells or invading organisms. They would have little or no effect on the normal, healthy cells of the body. Toward the end of his life, Ehrlich studied chemotherapy for cancer. In 1908 his work earned him the Nobel Prize for Medicine.

PAUL EHRLICH

LIVED: 1854–1915

NATIONALITY: German

FAMOUS FOR: Developing the first chemotherapy

DID YOU KNOW? Ehrlich wanted chemicals to work like "magic bullets" (as he called them), to seek out and destroy disease-causing agents in the body.

RADIATION

In the early 1900s, scientists were puzzled by X-rays and other kinds of radiation that they were discovering. Marie Curie explained the radiation as coming directly from atoms, which are the tiny particles that make up matter (anything that has substance and takes up space).

Curie discovered two of the elements (kinds of matter) that naturally give off this radiation. She also investigated the use of radiation to shrink or kill tumors, an idea called **radiation therapy**. With many changes, radiation therapy continues to be used today.

Unfortunately, high-energy radiation can be very dangerous to human health. Curie suffered poor health throughout her life because of her work.

MARIE CURIE

LIVED: 1867–1934

NATIONALITY: Polish (later, French)

FAMOUS FOR: Studying radioactivity; isolating and discovering radioactive elements; using radiation to treat disease

DID YOU KNOW? In World War I, Curie and her daughter Irene took X-rays of wounded soldiers. They often drove a van—called a Petit ("Little") Curie— to the battlefield!

TREATING CANCER TODAY

As recently as 40 years ago, doctors could offer no useful treatment for many types of cancer. Much has changed since then. New drugs, new treatments, and new ways to detect cancer have helped save many lives. Unfortunately, cancer continues to claim millions of lives every year.

CANCER RESEARCH

Doctors and scientists around the world have devoted their lives to finding new treatments and cures for cancer. So have many hospitals and organizations. In addition, many people who have survived cancer, such as United States cycling champion Lance Armstrong, donate their time and money to fighting the disease.

Much cancer research is devoted to identifying the causes of cancer. Some of these causes are chemicals in the environment called **carcinogens**. Chemicals in tobacco are well-known carcinogens. So is asbestos, a material that was once often used in building construction. Its use is now banned because it is a carcinogen.

Other cancer research involves new drugs and treatments. Doctors usually test their ideas on animals first, then on human cancer patients who volunteer. Drugs and treatments that prove successful may gradually become accepted.

After her own treatment for cancer in 2005, the Australian singer Kylie Minogue visited children with cancer in a local hospital.

ARUL M. CHINNAIYAN

Cancer involves changes in the cells of the body. Dr. Arul Chinnaiyan studies cancer at the level of cells. Why do some cells become cancerous and others do not? How does a cell change when it becomes cancerous? These are the kinds of questions that he and his team study at the University of Michigan in the United States.

Dr. Chinnaiyan has discovered many **biomarkers** of cancer. A biomarker is a chemical in the body that indicates a disease or the possibility of a disease. A biomarker could show that cancer could strike, or that it has already arrived. Dr. Chinnaiyan's hope is that by identifying useful biomarkers, doctors can discover cancer in a patient in an early stage. The earlier cancer is detected, the more likely it is that it can be cured.

Dr. Chinnaiyan also founded an organization to gather data from cancer researchers around the world. The organization runs an Internet site that helps scientists share their data and exchange ideas.

HEALTHY BABIES

When Virginia Apgar left school, she knew that she wanted to be a doctor. At the age of 24, she was one of the few women doctors of her time. She trained in surgery and in anesthesia (pain relief). Yet her major contribution—the Apgar Score—came in the field of infant care.

The Apgar Score is a method of evaluating an infant's health during the first few minutes after birth. It measures basic signs of health, including heart rate, breathing, muscle tone, reflexes, and skin color. Doctors value the Apgar Score because it can be measured quickly and it is very useful. If a newborn has pale, bluish skin, poor muscle tone, and a weak heartbeat, then doctors know that the baby needs immediate medical attention.

VIRGINIA APGAR

LIVED: 1909–1974

NATIONALITY: American

FAMOUS FOR: Developing a system for measuring the health of newborn infants

DID YOU KNOW? Apgar was the first professor of medicine to specialize in birth defects.

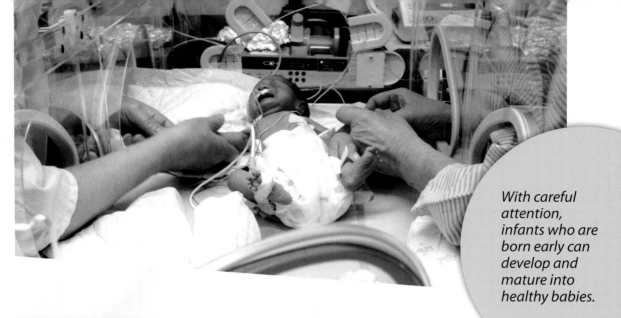

With careful attention, infants who are born early can develop and mature into healthy babies.

NEONATOLOGY

Babies usually stay inside their mother's body for about nine months before they are born. In some cases, however, babies are born early. If they are born especially early, babies need extra help to survive. A **neonatologist** is a doctor who treats newborn infants, especially those who are ill or born earlier than normal.

Neonatologists work in hospitals where babies are delivered. Under their care, babies born after only seven months have a good chance of surviving and leading a healthy life.

THEN

In the 1800s, even infants growing up in clean, healthy conditions often did not survive. Among poor people in crowded cities, about 300 of every 1,000 infants died before their first birthday.

NOW

Today, doctors and nurses are well trained to care for infants and their mothers. So are **midwives**, who are health care professionals that help women deliver babies. In the USA, Europe, and Australia, the death rate is less than 10 infants per 1,000 born.

Sports Medicine

To win a game or race, an athlete's body must be in peak condition. Athletes' muscles must be strong and durable, and so must their bones, heart, lungs, and other organs. People who work in the field of **sports medicine** help athletes to be as strong and healthy as they can be. They also help athletes recover from injuries.

KINESIOLOGY

Pitchers in professional baseball can throw a ball up to 100 miles (161 km) per hour. Other athletes can run 20 kilometers (12 miles) in about an hour. Weight lifters might try to lift 90 kilograms (200 pounds) above their heads.

What is the best way for the body to accomplish feats like these? How can the body work at its peak and still stay safe from injuries? These are questions that are studied in the field of **kinesiology**, the science of how the body moves. Experts in this field work with athletes to help them perfect their technique (way of doing something). They also work with people who have injured their muscles, bones, or nerves.

PEAK PERFORMERS

When professional athletes suffer serious injuries, they often call on Dr. James Andrews of Birmingham, Alabama. Famous football, basketball, and baseball players have been among his patients. He has successfully treated many professional players for injured shoulders, knees, and elbows.

Dr. Andrews does more than just perform operations (surgery). He is the founder of the American Sports Medicine Institute (ASMI). There, Dr. Andrews and his team of researchers carefully observe athletes as they perform the movements of their sport, such as running, leaping, kicking, throwing, or catching.

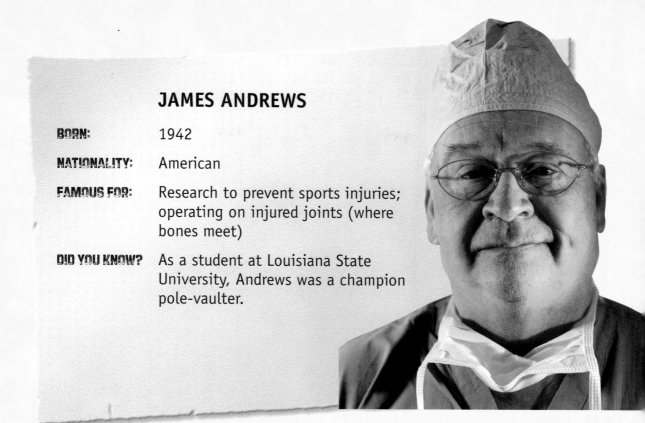

JAMES ANDREWS

BORN: 1942

NATIONALITY: American

FAMOUS FOR: Research to prevent sports injuries; operating on injured joints (where bones meet)

DID YOU KNOW? As a student at Louisiana State University, Andrews was a champion pole-vaulter.

At ASMI, they also take precise measurements of each athlete's body as it moves. By analyzing the data and applying their knowledge of muscles, bones, and joints, the team is able to recommend specific practices that help athletes perform at their peak while preventing injuries.

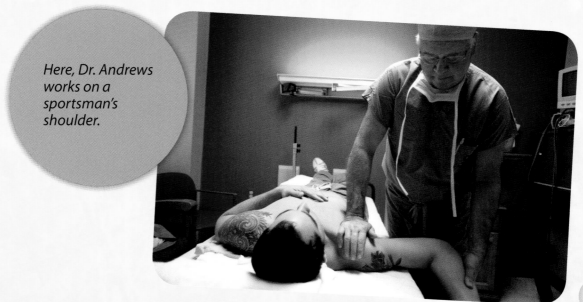

Here, Dr. Andrews works on a sportsman's shoulder.

Doctors Who Make a
DIFFERENCE

Every day, doctors, nurses, and other health care professionals treat a huge number of people all over the world. Each one of them makes a difference in the lives of their patients.

"I believe that education is the best tool to get out of poverty."

Koneru Prasad

DR. KONERU PRASAD

Dr. Koneru Prasad was born in India, but now lives and practices medicine in the United Kingdom. In 1992 Dr. Prasad donated his family's house in India to be a home for orphaned children. This was the beginning of a charity he founded called HEAL, which stands for Health and Education for All.

Dr. Prasad's goal is to provide health care, education, and other services for needy children in India. All of the staff at HEAL are volunteers.

U. DIANE BUCKINGHAM

U. Diane Buckingham began her career as a nurse. Then she identified a need in her community that was not being met. The need was for mental health care, especially for children and teenagers. After many years of training, Buckingham became a psychiatrist, which is a doctor who studies and treats disorders of the mind.

Today, Dr. Buckingham practices psychiatry in Kansas City, Kansas. Much of her work is with children and teenagers in the African-American community. She also speaks to doctors, students, parents, and schoolteachers. One of her lessons is that doctors must take account of their patients' culture and background. She also believes that educating people about mental health is the best way to help them stay healthy.

"I believe by educating your patients, you empower them for better health care."

U. Diane Buckingham

THE FLYING DOCTORS

Modern medical care is often scarce in eastern Africa, especially in remote villages. For many sick or injured Africans, a group called the Flying Doctors is often the difference between life and death. Calls for help come over the radio. Then the doctors are flown or driven to the rescue. They often treat animal bites or help deliver babies. The teams may also carry the severely wounded or sick to city hospitals.

Sometimes the work is dangerous. The Flying Doctors might be asked to travel to war zones to treat injured civilians. The doctors know that their work is very important. "The patients have nobody else," says Marlene Long, one of the doctors on the team. "You can't tell them to come back tomorrow, because there might be no tomorrow."

"These people live on less than a dollar a day, and asking them to pay is impossible. So we do it for nothing."

Alex Gikanda, a nurse with the Flying Doctors

Dr. Padilla believes in good health care for everyone. This is a free health and dental clinic in California.

DR. ADRIANA PADILLA

When Adriana Padilla was in college, she struggled to help her mother get the health care she needed. Her mother spoke only Spanish, while the doctors spoke only English. Padilla's experiences helped convince her to choose medicine as a career. She also chose medicine because she was good at science and math.

Today, Dr. Padilla is a family doctor in California, where she sees many patients from the Hispanic community. She also teaches medicine and speaks to community members. Her goal is to give all of her patients the quality health care they deserve.

"Listening, communicating, and caring, with just the right amount of lightheartedness, is my philosophy."

Adriana Padilla

The Future of Medicine

What will medicine be like in the future? New treatments or cures may be discovered, yet new diseases are likely to arise. Doctors are sure to continue benefiting from computers and other technology. Yet they will also rely on many old-fashioned skills, such as listening to their patients and drawing conclusions about their illnesses.

One prediction is bound to come true: doctors and nurses will continue to be needed wherever people live. Today, the health care needs of many people are not being met. As the human population grows, the need for medical care grows, too.

To become doctors, medical students must study health and medicine for many years.

CAREERS IN MEDICINE

Becoming a doctor or nurse requires long hours of study and practice. In college, future doctors must study science subjects such as biology, chemistry, and physics. Then comes four years of medical school, followed by years of training in a hospital. Even when doctors begin practicing medicine, they are expected to keep up to date with new medical knowledge and discoveries.

Would you be interested in a career in medicine? If you are willing to study and work hard, then the medical community would welcome you. Doctors, nurses, and other health care professionals have hard jobs, but they gain the satisfaction of helping people lead happier, healthier lives.

ROBOT SURGERY?

These days, robots are used to assemble cars, mow lawns, and even explore space. But could robots ever perform surgery? Many doctors and scientists think so. In fact, robots already assist surgeons in a few hospitals.

If the technology is perfected, robot surgeons would have certain advantages over human ones. They would never tire during long operations. They could cut and stitch tissues very precisely. And, if necessary, they could be monitored or controlled from far away.

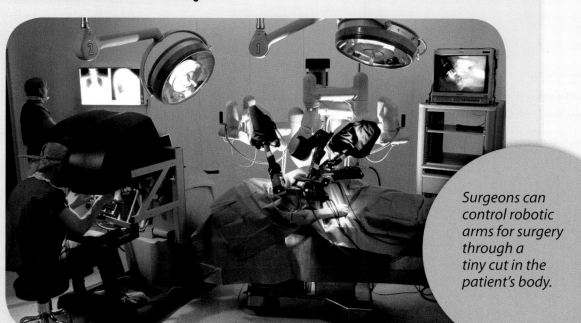

Surgeons can control robotic arms for surgery through a tiny cut in the patient's body.

TIMELINE

Follow the colored arrows to see how some of the ideas and discoveries of medical scientists influenced other scientists.

1796
Edward Jenner tested his idea that cowpox could prevent smallpox, which led to the first vaccine.

1859
Louis Pasteur showed how germs reproduce. Later he developed vaccines against many infections.

1865
Joseph Lister used carbolic acid to create antiseptic (germ-free) conditions during surgery.

1854
An outbreak of cholera killed thousands of people in London. John Snow showed that contaminated water was the cause.

1909
Paul Ehrlich developed the first form of chemotherapy.

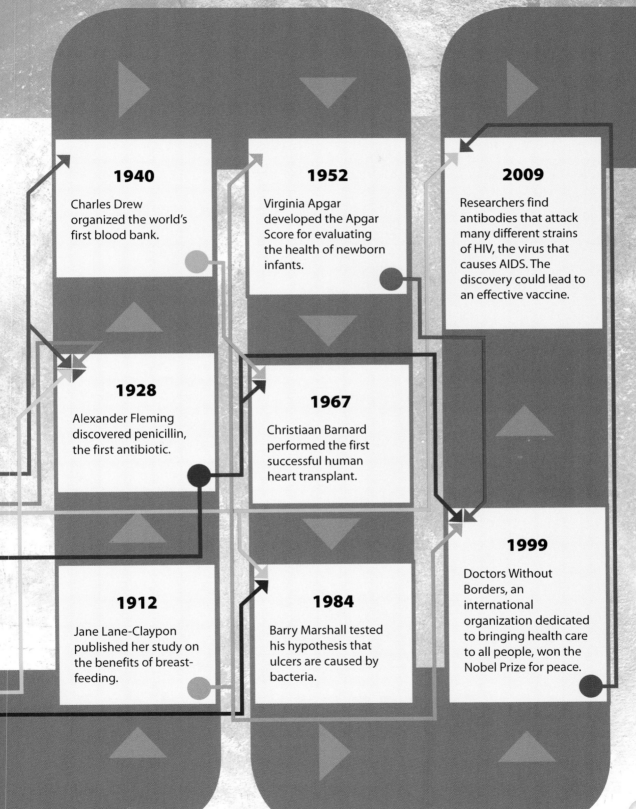

1940

Charles Drew organized the world's first blood bank.

1952

Virginia Apgar developed the Apgar Score for evaluating the health of newborn infants.

2009

Researchers find antibodies that attack many different strains of HIV, the virus that causes AIDS. The discovery could lead to an effective vaccine.

1928

Alexander Fleming discovered penicillin, the first antibiotic.

1967

Christiaan Barnard performed the first successful human heart transplant.

1999

Doctors Without Borders, an international organization dedicated to bringing health care to all people, won the Nobel Prize for peace.

1912

Jane Lane-Claypon published her study on the benefits of breast-feeding.

1984

Barry Marshall tested his hypothesis that ulcers are caused by bacteria.

Glossary

AIDS short for **a**cquired **i**mmune **d**eficiency **s**yndrome, a deadly disease that attacks the body's ability to fight infections

anesthesia pain relief

antibiotic drug that fights infections from bacteria

antiseptic germ-free; also medicine used to prevent a wound from being infected

bacteria tiny, single-celled living things only visible with a microscope; a type of germ

biomarker chemical in the body that signals a disease or predicts the arrival of a disease

blood bank storage facility for blood and blood products

cancer general term for many diseases in which cells grow abnormally and rapidly, harming the body

carcinogen chemical in the environment that can cause cancer

cell tiny unit visible with a microscope that makes up all living things

chemical substance found as a solid, liquid, or gas. A chemical may occur naturally or be made in a factory.

chemotherapy use of chemicals to treat disease

cholera deadly disease that affects the digestive tract

drug substance that changes how the body functions

element substance that consists of only one kind of molecule

fungi group of living things that include mushrooms, yeasts, and molds

germ tiny living or nonliving thing that can cause disease

HIV short for **h**uman **i**mmunodeficiency **v**irus, the virus that causes AIDS

hypothesis logical prediction or guess that can be tested

kinesiology study of how the body moves

matter substance that physical objects are made of

medicine substance that changes the way the body functions

midwife health care professional who helps women deliver babies

mutate change into a new form

neonatologist doctor who treats newborn infants

Nobel Prize international award given each year for physics, chemistry, physiology or medicine, literature, and peace

pasteurization process of slightly heating milk or other food to kill germs or slow down their activity

penicillin first antibiotic, used to fight infections from bacteria

radiation therapy use of high-energy radiation, such as X-rays and gamma rays, to treat cancer and other diseases

smallpox deadly disease in which the patient suffers skin rashes and a high fever, now eliminated due to worldwide vaccination

sports medicine the field of medicine devoted to helping athletes prevent and recover from injuries

sterile free of germs

surgery procedure in which the body is opened and treated

tumor clump of cancerous cells

ulcer sore caused by a break in the skin or lining, such as of the stomach or small intestine

vaccine treatment that prevents a type of germ from infecting the body by using a small amount of it, so that the body builds resistance

virus nonliving germ

X-ray photograph of bones and other parts inside the body, taken using rays that can go through solid matter

yeast single-celled form of fungus

Find Out More

Books

Coad, John. *Finding Better Medicines* (Why Science Matters). Chicago: Heinemann Library, 2009.

Fandel, Jennifer. *Louis Pasteur and Pasteurization* (Graphic Library: Inventions and Discovery). Chicago: Raintree, 2011.

Glasscock, Sarah. *How Nurses Use Math* (Math in the Real World). New York: Chelsea House, 2009.

Miller, Connie. *Marie Curie and Radioactivity* (Graphic Library: Inventions and Discovery). Chicago: Raintree, 2011.

Morgan, Sally. *Fighting Infectious Diseases* (Science at the Edge, 2nd edition). Chicago: Heinemann Library, 2009.

Websites

Find out more about Doctors Without Borders and the work they do worldwide:
www.doctorswithoutborders.org

For more information about the Apgar Score and how it is used to test newborn babies:
kidshealth.org/parent/newborn/first_days/apgar.html

Check out the World Health Organization's website for more information about vaccination programs and major medical breakthroughs:
www.who.int/en

A great source for reliable, up-to-date information on topics related to medicine:
www.mayo.edu

For more information about the deadly disease cholera:
www.nhs.uk/Conditions/Cholera/Pages/Definition.aspx

Place to visit

National Museum of Health and Medicine
6900 Georgia Avenue, NW, Building 54
Washington, DC 20307
Tel: 202-782-2200
nmhm.washingtondc.museum

This museum includes medical instruments and artifacts and focuses on the history and practice of American medicine, military medicine, and current medical research. It has many medical instruments and artifacts, as well as a 3-D hologram of the human body.

Topics to research

Animals
Find out the arguments for and against using animals in medical research. What are your own conclusions about this?

A disease-free world
Smallpox was eradicated (wiped out) throughout the world in 1980. Diseases can be eradicated if enough people take part in vaccination programs. Find out what vaccinations are available through your school or in your area.

Public health
Health care can be very expensive. In the United States, most people pay into a private health insurance system that pays just for their own health care. In countries such as the United Kingdom, all working people put money into a national health service fund that is used to meet the cost of everyone's health care needs. In other countries, people pay directly for their own health care. Which system do you think is best? How important is it that everyone has good health care? What should people do if they cannot afford to pay for health care?

Transplants
Check out the history of transplant surgery, from the first heart transplant in 1967 to the full-face transplants of the 21st century.

Index

AIDS 8, 16–17, 43
American Sports Medicine Institute (ASMI) 34–35
anesthesia 24
Andrews, James 34–35
antibiotics 8, 9, 10, 12, 43
antibodies 43
antiseptic conditions 18, 42
Apgar Score 32, 43
Apgar, Virginia 32, 43
artificial limbs 22
asbestos 30
aspirin 10
athletes 34–35

bacteria 6, 8, 9, 10, 12, 14, 24
Barnard, Christiaan 20–21, 43
Bekker, Linda-Gail 17
Benjamin, Regina 27
biomarkers 31
"bleeding" (treatment) 5
blood banks 19, 43
blood donations 19
brain surgery 23
breastfeeding 26
Buckingham, U. Diane 37

cancer 28–31
carcinogens 30
careers in medicine 41
Chain, Ernst 11, 12
chemotherapy 28, 42
Chinnaiyan, Arul M. 31
cholera 6, 24–25, 42
colds and flu 6, 8, 16
cowpox 15
Curie, Marie 29

digitalis 10
diphtheria 16
Doctors Without Borders 27, 43
Drew, Charles 19, 43
drug resistance 12
drugs 10–13

ear infections 6
education 36, 37
Ehrlich, Paul 28, 42
eye surgery 23

Fleming, Alexander 10, 11, 12, 43
Florey, Howard 11, 12
Flying Doctors 38
fungi 6, 10

germs 6–8, 18, 26, 42
Gikanda, Alex 38
Gobbo, Grace 13
Goodall, Jane 13

HEAL 36
heart transplants 20–21, 43
HIV 8, 17, 43
hole in the heart 20
hygiene 8, 18
hypotheses 9, 15

immune system 16
infant care 26, 32–33

Jenner, Edward 14, 15, 42

kinesiology 34

Lane-Claypon, Janet 26, 43
lasers 23
Leeuwenhoek, Anton van 6
Lister, Joseph 18, 42
Long, Marlene 38

malaria 16
Marshall, Barry 9, 43
measles 16
mental health care 37
microscopes 6
midwives 33

neonatalogists 33
Nobel Prize 9, 11, 27, 28

Obama, Barack 27

Padilla, Adriana 39
Pasteur, Louis 6, 7, 18, 42
pasteurization 7
penicillin 10–11, 12, 43
plant medicines 10, 13
polio 16
poverty 26, 27, 36, 38
Prasad, Koneru 36
psychiatry 37
public health 24–27
public health officials 26

radiation therapy 29
rain forests 12
robot surgery 41
rubella 16

smallpox 6, 14, 15, 42
Snow, John 24, 25, 42
sore throat 6
sports medicine 34–35
sterile conditions 8
stomach ulcers 9
surgery 18–23, 41

tobacco 30
tooth decay 6
transplant surgery 20–21
tumors 20, 23, 28, 29

ulcers 9, 43

vaccines 7, 14–17, 26, 42
viruses and viral infections 6, 8, 14, 16

war zones 27, 38
Warren, Robin 9
water supplies 25, 26
women in health care 13, 17, 26, 27, 29, 32, 37, 38, 39
World Health Organization 14
wound infection 18

X-rays 29